"This small group resource takes men on a journey toward the freedom only humility can bring: freedom from pride, from insecurity, and from the torment of comparative thinking. Take the challenge—you won't regret it."

Brad Hambrick, Pastor of Counseling, The Summit Church; author of *Transformative Friendships*

"This study gives men a new way of seeing humility, and it's a gift. Ed Welch takes a concept that you thought you understood and makes it three-dimensional."

Marc Davis, Associate Area Director for Renewal, Serge

"Ed Welch offers wise love at its finest in this study. The nastiness of pride is unmasked, and the manliness of humility is unveiled. I can't wait to invite the men I shepherd to join me on this path."

Greg Norfleet, Director of Counseling Ministry, Briarwood Presbyterian Church

"While pride is always lurking and luring us, it is the humility of Christ that truly captures the heart. Humility is the way of the Christian because it is the way of Christ."

Nathan Sawyer, Pastor, Grace Church Memphis; online instructor, CCEF

"This is a gem of a study, filled with wisdom. Ed traces the silent thread of humility (or its lack) through our sins and our virtues. It might be written for men, but it's for everyone!"

Paul E. Miller, Author of *A Praying Church* and *J-Curve: Dying and Rising With Christ in Everyday Life*

"In a world where humility often feels scarce, Ed Welch offers men a rich, grace-filled invitation to rediscover this vital virtue. Drawing from years of counseling experience and deep biblical insight, he helps participants see humility not as weakness but as

Christlikeness—continually lifting our eyes to Jesus, the true model of a humble heart."

Jonathan D. Holmes, Interim Executive Director, CCEF

"This is vintage Ed Welch. In this study guide, things we thought we knew about pride and humility are revisited in ways that draw participants into personal engagement with Christ. This is a humility project that will bless your soul."

Steve Midgley, Executive Director, Biblical Counselling UK

"Ed Welch shepherds us gently toward our humble Savior. This study guide is a timely gift to the church—inviting us to slow down, listen, and live more like the One who is gentle and lowly in heart."

Robert K. Cheong, Executive Director, Gospel Care Ministries; author of *Restore: Changing How We Live and Love* and *Restoration Story: Why Jesus Matters in a Broken World*

THE HUMILITY PROJECT FOR MEN STUDY GUIDE

THE HUMILITY PROJECT FOR MEN STUDY GUIDE

THE WAY TO STRENGTH, HONOR, AND CONTENTMENT

Edward T. Welch

New Growth Press, Greensboro, NC 27401
newgrowthpress.com

Cover Design: Tim Green
Interior Typesetting and Ebook: Lisa Parnell, lparnellbookservices.com

ISBN: 978-1-64507-595-0 (print)
ISBN: 978-1-64507-596-7 (ebook)

Printed in Colombia

30 29 28 27 26 1 2 3 4 5

CONTENTS

INTRODUCTION
WHAT IS THE HUMILITY PROJECT?

The truly human life is lived "with all humility" (Ephesians 4:2). It is the path of rest, wisdom, honor, and love. The only alternative? Pride. You find it in holding grudges, being right, needing the approval of others, and wanting to be just a little more respected, a little more important. The challenge is that pride is natural to us. Humility will take some work.

The project in front of you requires you to band together, aspire to humility before God, help each other fight against the pride that insists on clinging to us all, grow in ways that are obvious to those close to you, and be a light to the world. All in eight meetings.

GETTING STARTED

Eight sessions together is not much time when the movement from pride to humility is among the most ambitious changes we could ever consider. But from the vantage point of lives that are already hard and busy, it is a lot. Those meetings—and the work done between them—will give you an opportunity to grow, and you can be sure that your friends and family will be happy to release you from whatever you might miss during the weeks ahead.

Our purpose. Humility is God's desire for us. The project before you is to understand what Scripture means by *humility* and *pride*, and then to find that pride, battle it, and enjoy humbly walking with God through life.

The vibe. The work in front of you will try to follow both what Jesus says and how he says it. Life with him, in his house and his kingdom, has a particular feel. This is one reason that you are banding together. Jesus brings people together, and he uses our words to help each other, as "iron sharpens iron" (Proverbs 27:17). He is pleased when we gather for his purposes. You can be sure that he speaks a blessing over your time, which means that he is determined to benefit you and your relationships.

Since people talk when they gather, you won't be surprised that life with Jesus includes lots of talking. His house is *not* about monastic silence. Instead, he talks and you respond; then you talk and he responds. Then you talk to others, listening and responding to them, and occasionally one person is so excited that they talk to everyone and we all respond. Talk to God. Talk to your family and friends. Talk to those at work. And listen as others talk. There is a lot of talking and listening and responding in God's house.

As a way to get into that groove, go ahead and respond to the readings—both the ones in this study guide and the ones you'll do on your own in the devotional. Say, "Amen," "What?" "Impossible!" or whatever is on your mind. Raucous is good; it is humility's lesser-known style. Also, when you read words in bold letters, speak them together. It is a reminder that God enjoys hearing from you.

If you are unfamiliar with how Jesus does things, or if you are new to it all, think of this as a kind of open house where Jesus himself invites you in. As you walk around, everything should look better than what you expected and more like the home you always wanted.

WHAT WILL YOU DO ON THIS JOURNEY?

As with most things, the more work you do, the more you and others will benefit. Here's what you'll be doing as you embark on the Humility Project:

- Attend the eight group meetings.
- This study guide will lead you through these meetings. The plan for each week looks like this:
    - Discuss some general questions to get warmed up.
    - Read about the key idea.

    - Do an exercise on your own, and then discuss your findings with the group.
    - Read the article on a particular aspect of humility, marking anything that strikes you, and discuss the questions following it.
    - Read Scripture responsively.
    - Pray together.
- Do the assignments in the "Up Ahead" section (listed near the end of every session except the last one). These will include reading the week's devotions from *The Humility Project for Men: The Way to Honor, Strength, and Contentment*, as well as being prepared to talk about them together and enlisting someone to pray for you.

Please enter. Talk. Work hard, and enjoy the fruit of that labor.

A Word to Group Leaders

Please share the information in the "What Will You Do on This Journey?" section with the group before the first meeting.

MEETING 1
KNOWING HUMILITY

OPENERS *(7 minutes)*

- What words or associations do you think pop into people's minds when they hear the words *humble* and *humility*? Consider characters from books, movies, and television shows.
- What do you think of when you hear the words *humble* and *humility*—both good and bad?

KEY IDEA *(3 minutes)*

Saint Augustine knew that humility is at the very center of the life that knows Jesus. He put it this way: "I wish you to prepare for yourself no other way of seizing and holding the truth than that which has been prepared by Him who, as God, saw the weakness of our goings. In that way the first part is humility; the second, humility; the third, humility."[1]

But what does humility mean? *Humility means holding fast to the reality that Jesus is Lord and I am not. It means living before God, dependent on him, with a listening, teachable heart.*

Humility is on God's heart for us, so we want to find out what he says about it. We'll consider what Jesus says and how he says it, and we'll look to the Spirit to help us understand these things and reflect them in our lives. As you learn about humility and embody it more and more, you will notice a growing gentleness and strength, and others will notice *something* is different.

ARTICLE *(5 minutes)*

What Humility Is, and What Humility Is Not

Instructions:

- *Read the article aloud, taking turns at the paragraph breaks. If you prefer not to read, say "Pass," and the next person will begin reading.*
- *Sentences in* **boldface** *are for the whole group to read aloud together. Awkward? A little. But worth trying as a way to say that you are in this together. Wait until the second meeting before you decide against it.*
- *If anything from the reading stands out to you, circle, underline, or highlight it. If a question occurs to you, jot it down. After the reading, you'll have an opportunity to share your observations and questions.*

We are starting on a project to grow in humility. Why is it worth our time and effort? The Lord says to us, "I dwell in the high and holy place, and also with him who is of a contrite and lowly spirit" (Isaiah 57:15). This means that here on earth, God dwells *only* with the humble. His life and power exist only in the humble. A wise man, under the Spirit's guidance, said, "The reward for humility and fear of the LORD is riches and honor and life" (Proverbs 22:4). No humility, no riches and no honor. This makes humility sound good, if not necessary, but you might also wonder if there are easier ways to riches and honor.

You come to this group with various thoughts about humility. Some are accurate and some less so. As you go through the next several weeks, your view of humility will gradually be refined. The refining process can begin with this foundational truth: If God calls us to humility, and Jesus lived it out, then it is very good.

That doesn't mean it will be easy. Pride is natural to us; humility is not. We might be tempted to think that we are humble if we are more reserved or less reactive when criticized, but humility is not a personality style. Whether we are quiet or aggressive by nature, humility is a gift from the Spirit that is learned and practiced.

There is not just one definition of humility, but every definition should include these two basic features: living under God and listening.

First, humility lives under God. You might think that humility is about being a nice, modest person while someone else isn't. But Scripture leads in a different direction. Scripture is first about humility before God. That should be a relief and sound fairly easy. He is God, after all, and you are not. Jesus is now the reigning King. In all ways and at all times, you live under him. That simply means that you live before God—always in his presence—and you walk *with* him. The important thing is that there is no getting away from God. Even when you consider what humility looks like before people, remember that humility is first before God. Everything begins there.

Who is the Lord? He is the triune God—Father, Son, Spirit—who is great and good. We will use those two qualities of God to organize the many things that he reveals about himself. He is the great God over all. *The* God formed *you*, and the creation belongs to the Creator. Yet his greatness is crammed with his goodness. The Father determined that the Son would die on our behalf, so that the Spirit would bring us close to him, because that is what you do with those that you love. He knew you before you were born, and he loved you. He knew you by name, and he has revealed that he alone is the God of steadfast love. You exist because he wanted you. That is good, and it's humbling. All this has been revealed to us through Jesus, the King.

Now let's make our first attempt to respond as a group:

Jesus, you are great and you are good.

Speaking is a step past mere thinking, and it will keep you awake.

Second, humility listens. As we live under and before God, we are busy worshiping, obeying, honoring, representing, asking questions, and doing much more. *Listening* is the way to coordinate those many responses. Listening learns from God and always does something in response. You never merely learn a new fact about Christ. You learn and speak, learn and obey, learn and give thanks.

Humility means that you live before God, dependent on him, with a listening, teachable heart.

This will get us started. It means that you hear God's voice over the opinions of other people, over your own contrary desires, over the guilt of your past, and over the voices that humiliate you and pronounce you worthless. Such listening, of course, is decidedly not easy, and the Spirit will help you.

How will you discern God's voice from the competition's?

- His words keep coming back to Jesus—what Jesus says, how he lived, and what he has done for you.
- His words have certain cadences and rhythms. For example, humility is first before God, then before others. Humility is first what you receive from Jesus and then how you respond to him.
- His words sound good, surprisingly good.
- His words invite you to both listen carefully and respond to him.

As you put on humility, you will notice some things and not notice others.

- You will *not* notice *yourself*—at least not as much. You will be more comfortable with your strengths and weaknesses, and less prone to hide your sins and your neediness.
- You will notice that you are able to rest, with less effort given to being self-protective and being "somebody."
- You will notice people—their stories, their joys, their sorrows.
- You will notice that people are what make life rich, just as God intended.

Humility should *not* feel like humiliation or shame. Humiliation is when you have been disgraced and laid low by another, and shame is when you believe you really are disgraceful. Humility is walking with the Servant-King for the good of others. In that dependent relationship, we have decisions to make about how to respond to the wickedness and oppression that we and others have experienced. These will not be one-size-fits-all responses, but instead will take into account the particular circumstances. Humility universally takes away our reasons to hide and be silent, and humility resists being defined by the wicked acts done against us.

In short, humility should feel like freedom. You are settled. Not striving. Not hiding. Not defending. Humility yields confidence that what your Father says is true—your past sins are forgiven and far from him, and your regrets and failures cannot nullify his good plans.

DISCUSSION *(15 minutes)*

What stands out or surprises you from this article?

Does it bring up any questions?

Humility means that you live before God, dependent on him, with a listening, teachable heart. That definition has three related parts: You live before God's face, you need him, and your life depends on hearing his words to you and living them out. Imagine one way this could be expressed in daily life.

EXERCISE *(20 minutes)*

Instructions: Read the verses and answer the questions on your own. Then, discuss as a group what you found.

Below are several verses that appear in the devotion for Day 1. Each verse reflects an aspect of humility. Choose two that stand out to you.

- ☐ "Jesus is Lord." (Romans 10:9)
- ☐ "Speak [Lord], for your servant is listening." (1 Samuel 3:10 NIV)
- ☐ "Every good and perfect gift is from above." (James 1:17 NIV)
- ☐ "My soul finds rest in God alone." (Psalm 62:1 NIV 2008)
- ☐ "He [Jesus] must increase, but I must decrease." (John 3:30)
- ☐ "As for me, I am poor and needy, but the Lord takes thought for me." (Psalm 40:17)

Why did you choose these two verses?

How does each one guide you toward a humble heart?

Take a few minutes to share which verses you selected and why.

RESPONSIVE READING AND QUESTIONS *(15 minutes)*

Instructions:

- *Psalm 40 is a useful guide to humility. Read it responsively, with one man reading the words in italics, another reading the regular text, and the entire group reading the* ***boldface text*** *together.*
- *As you read, keep these features in mind:*
  - *Jesus is all through the psalm, which follows the pattern of faith: Our hearts turn and see what Jesus has done, and then we respond.*
  - *The psalmist is very open with his private thoughts.*
  - *There is a lot of talking.*
  - *Remember those last words: "I am poor and needy."*
- *As you read, circle, underline, or highlight things that are important to you.*

ఌ ఌ ఌ

The psalm begins: First, you speak about Jesus.

I waited patiently for the Lord;
he inclined to me and heard my cry.
(Jesus always listens and acts.)
He drew me up from the pit of destruction,
out of the miry bog,
and set my feet upon a rock,
making my steps secure.
(Jesus has already secured this in his death and resurrection for you.)

Now Jesus joins in with you. The psalms often have different voices, and it is not unusual for those voices to join in with yours. In this case, Jesus speaks with you in this next section. He speaks from his own experience.

Blessed is the man
who makes the Lord his trust,
who does not turn to the proud,
to those who go astray after a lie!

You have multiplied, O Lord my God,
your wondrous deeds and your thoughts toward us;
none can compare with you!
I will proclaim and tell of them,
yet they are more than can be told.
In sacrifice and offering you have not delighted,
but you have given me an open ear.
(There it is: Humility is being teachable before God; he opens your ears to hear.)
Burnt offering and sin offering
you have not required.
(He wants you to listen, receive, and trust. You do not wait until you have a perfect sacrifice before you come to him.)

Jesus speaks. The "I" in this section is Jesus talking about himself. Hear what he says.

Then I said, "Behold, I have come;
in the scroll of the book it is written of me:
I delight to do your will, O my God;
your law is within my heart."
I have told the glad news of deliverance
in the great congregation;
behold, I have not restrained my lips,
as you know, O Lord.

Now you speak.

As for you, O Lord, you will not restrain
your mercy from me;
your steadfast love and your faithfulness will
ever preserve me!
For evils have encompassed me
beyond number;
my iniquities have overtaken me,
and I cannot see;
they are more than the hairs of my head;
my heart fails me.

You make your request.

Be pleased, O LORD, to deliver me!
O LORD, make haste to help me!

Your request gets big.

But may all who seek you
rejoice and be glad in you;
may those who love your salvation
say continually, **"Great is the LORD!"**

You end with the words of the wise.

As for me, I am poor and needy,
but the Lord takes thought for me.
You are my help and my deliverer;
do not delay, O my God!

"Poor and needy" refers first to your own sins, and then to the injustices done against you, and then to the burdens of life. The first category—your sins—is more serious because they can separate you from God. The sins of other people do not have that power. Psalm 40 pronounces deliverance from both: Your sins are forgiven now; your deliverance is unfolding even now.

QUESTIONS

You were asked to mark what was important to you. What did you mark and why? What are your initial reflections on the psalm?

Author Eugene Peterson says the psalms are expert at "unselfing" us[2]—they redirect our attention away from ourselves and toward the Lord. How does this psalm lead you into humility and away from pride?

PRAY *(5 minutes)*

Pray together that you would know God as great and good and that you would see yourselves as living your lives under him. Pray that the Holy Spirit would give each of you a teachable heart that listens and responds to God's Word.

UP AHEAD *(5 minutes)*

This is what is ahead in the coming week:

1. Complete the "Put It Together" section below as soon as you can, while your memory of this time is fresh.
2. If you haven't already read the introduction to this study guide, go ahead and read it.

3. Between now and the next meeting, read these parts of *The Humility Project for Men* devotional: "Welcome," and the devotions for Day 1 through Day 7. It is all the better if you can read the devotions aloud with one other person. Speaking is good. Each reading is followed by a response. Please don't skip that part.
4. Ask one person outside the group to pray for you.
   - Communicate with the person in the next 48 hours.
   - Tell the person about the project in front of you. For example, "Pray for open ears and a heart that is willing to talk."
   - Send them a text after each of the coming meetings. Include one thing you are learning or one request for prayer.
5. Talk to *someone* about your humility project—a roommate, friend, spouse, child.
6. Be prepared to mention at the next meeting one thing from the devotions that has been important to you. Part of being all ears is wanting to learn from one another.

PUT IT TOGETHER

How would you summarize your time in the project so far? What can you tell others about your humility project?

MEETING 2
KNOWING PRIDE

OPENERS *(10 minutes)*

- What from this week's reading in the devotional has been important to you?
- What would you say a *proud person* looks like? What does someone who is filled with pride believe? Think? Do?

KEY IDEA

Pride is a kind of master category for all sin. It is tied to our old foes—the world, the flesh, and the devil—and like them, it leads to the darkness of death.

ARTICLE *(5 minutes)*

A Description of Pride

Instructions:

- *Read the article aloud, taking turns at the paragraph breaks. If you prefer not to read, say "Pass," and the next person will begin reading.*
- *Sentences in **boldface** are for the whole group to read aloud together.*
- *If anything from the reading stands out to you, circle, underline, or highlight it. If a question occurs to you, jot it down in the margins. After the reading, you will have an opportunity to share your observations and questions if you wish.*

"When pride comes, then comes disgrace,
but with the humble is wisdom." (Proverbs 11:2)

Pride is deadly. Look at your relational disasters of the past year. Pride is there. Notice the resentments, regrets, arguments, lies, and way too much time spent thinking about personal achievements and the opinions of others. Pride is right there. You know it has messed up your life, and yet we are odd people who still hold onto it.

An addict had been of two minds about following Jesus. Sometimes he asked, "Where can I turn other than Jesus?" At other times he whispered, "No way will I give up my booze." When he was asked, "What are you hearing from God today?" he answered truthfully, "Yes, I want Jesus at the center of my life. . . . I want to do what he says and not merely listen. But, man, is this difficult for me. I am realizing I am way more prideful and stubborn than I'd like to admit." *That* is spiritual power.

Pride is a friend of death.
It is weakness. Anyone can do it.
Humility is power as God's Spirit works in us.

Pride is more complicated than humility. It is actually part of a consortium of powers united by their partnership with death. *Pride listens to the world, the flesh, and the devil.* Together, these powers lie and prefer the cover of darkness. Like addictive drugs, they hope that you will come to love this path before you see that it's killing you.

The apostle John describes these forces as "the desires of the flesh and the desires of the eyes and pride of life" (1 John 2:16). He doesn't use the phrase "the world, the flesh and the devil," but he certainly identifies them. In other parts of this letter, he writes that Jesus appeared "to destroy the works of the devil" (3:8)—all of the powers arrayed against us.

In discussing this confederation, John first addresses the heart of pride, a.k.a., *the desires of the flesh*, or just, *the flesh. Flesh* can mean our general bent toward all kinds of sin, but John usually uses it to refer specifically to the human body and its desires. Someone who is lured by "the desires of the flesh," in John's use of the phrase, is a person whose heart is fixed on their own physical pleasures. What do you *really* want? Whatever your body and its desires tell you. This can get tricky because your physical desires are not necessarily evil. However, the good desires for food, sex, clothes, shelter, rest, and the absence of pain become "desires of the flesh" when they no longer live under God's words. *If Jesus is not first on your list of desires, the desires of the flesh will be.*

Following these desires of the flesh means a gradual descent into darkness. More precisely, the death that accompanies pride is gradual and subtle. Let's say you acknowledge God and even think well of him. You pray at some meals. But your daily life is about what is seen and earthbound—your obligations, how much you have, your interests, and who or what relieves your desires.

Your desires flirt with boundaries and eventually cross them. For example, you *think* about a sexual relationship, but you don't touch, so you think you are okay. Then you find porn, but you are still not touching, so you think you could be worse off. And so it goes. John Calvin has an insightful phrase for this: "Worldly men are intent on their own convenience."[3] That nails us quite nicely. Fleshly desires that are obvious are addictions; the less obvious are conveniences. Find these conveniences in things you believe you deserve or have earned—"me time," respect, recognition, mindless affection for anything on screens, the right to disregard boundaries in your heart or act out behaviors that are getting hard to justify.

Next on John's list is *the desires of the eyes*. These are the temptations around you that can satisfy a desire. This is also known as *the* world. Women, men, having a certain kind of body, cars, resumes, money, stuff. What do you *look* at? Jesus talks about this when he says, "if your eye is bad, your whole body will be full of darkness" (Matthew 6:23). We often use the word *world* to mean the earth. But here it's a kind of chorus of the flesh that promises real life. It says we will find satisfaction only in those things that we can see, and in our pride we believe this lie.

Last is *the pride of life*, which covers it all. Pride is a kind of master category for all that goes wrong with us. It says, "nothing is above me and my desires." It includes our physical desires but emphasizes how we desire reputation and being a little better than the next guy. It wants what it wants. Ironically, it is a slave to those desires. It always needs more. It is also a slave to other people—their achievements and opinions. Pride is never free.

As we move into humility, pride is always close by. *Always.* Just because you feel worthless doesn't mean pride is not always knocking at the door. Sometimes worthlessness comes on us because we want to be somebody and we are not—notice the pride sneaking in. Sometimes shame listens to our past more than to the words of Jesus—pride sneaks in there too. For human beings, all this comes prepackaged and doesn't have to be learned. It is like breathing.

We find pride in Jesus's disciples, even as he tells them about the death he will face in Jerusalem, where they are headed together for the last time: "A dispute also arose among [the disciples], as to which of them was to be regarded as the greatest" (Luke 22:24). Pride wants to be somebody, or at least more somebody than somebody else. It can look very religious because it wants to look good to the world. It can look like niceness. But in private it starts looking ugly.

In Scripture, the Pharisees are the prototype of pride. They were the ones who were considered most religious. They dressed better, prayed better, read Scripture longer, and assumed that God liked them more than others. But they lived for their own reputation. They compared themselves to others and thought they fared well. *This should scare you to death,* because this pride is in you.

How does pride feel? Whereas humility knows rest, pride is fidgety and agitated. You feel as though you are right. Other people? Not so much. You are easily inconvenienced because you are busy with your own desires. You are slow to apologize. All these attitudes are easy to see in other people, of course, but pride leaves us with personal blind spots.

To know humility is to be equally skilled at knowing its enemy.

DISCUSSION *(15 minutes)*

The article states, "Pride is a kind of master category for all that goes wrong with us." How would you explain to someone that all sin has pride at its core?

Since prides hides, let's take some time to unearth it: How would you define or describe your pride? Try to be specific. Look especially for those "conveniences," when you take the easy way and ignore the words of Jesus. Take a few minutes to think and jot down some notes, and then discuss with the group.

What else stood out to you as we read the article? What questions did you have?

EXERCISE *(20 minutes)*

Instructions: For at least two of the three settings below, write down a kind of conflict you have been involved in or have observed or heard about. Consider the situation and identify how pride contributed to the conflict. Then imagine how things would have gone differently if the people involved had shown humility.

Setting	What happened?	What role did pride play in this situation?	How would the situation have looked different if people had shown humility?
Among Family Members			
In the Workplace or at School			
Among Friends or in a Social Setting			

Now take a few minutes to discuss.

RESPONSIVE READING AND QUESTIONS *(15 minutes)*

Instructions:

- *Read the following responsively, with a leader (a volunteer or the group's facilitator) reading the regular text and the entire group reading the* ***boldface text*** *together. You do not need to read the Bible references in parentheses.*
- *As you read, circle, underline, or highlight things that are important to you.*

ᔕ ᔕ ᔕ

In our pride, we resist depending on God for everything we need and thanking him for all that we have. "What do you have that you did not receive?" (1 Corinthians 4:7)

Lord, help us remember that we are "poor and needy." (Psalm 40:17)

We are like the disciples; we compare ourselves to others, wanting to be "regarded as the greatest." (Luke 22:24)

Lord, help us to live in a way that is fitting for followers of the King, who "came not to be served but to serve." (Matthew 20:28)

"For by the grace given to me I say to everyone among you not to think of himself more highly than he ought to think, but to think with sober judgment, each according to the measure of faith that God has assigned." (Romans 12:3)

"Let love be genuine. Abhor what is evil; hold fast to what is good. Love one another with brotherly affection. Outdo one another in showing honor." (Romans 12:9–10)

"Rejoice with those who rejoice, weep with those who weep." (Romans 12:15)

"Live in harmony with one another. Do not be proud, but be willing to associate with people of low position. Do not be conceited." (Romans 12:16 NIV)

Scripture promises us this:

> **"God opposes the proud but gives grace to the humble."** (James 4:6)
>
> **"Pride brings a person low,**
> **but the lowly in spirit gain honor."** (Proverbs 29:23 NIV)

QUESTIONS

All pride is ultimately before God. For example, we want our own way, not his. We trust in ourselves, not him. Take one expression of pride and connect it to pride before God.

You were asked to circle, underline, or highlight what was important to you. What did you mark and why? What are your initial reflections on this reading?

PRAY *(5 minutes)*

Take time to confess the pride you see. Acknowledge your dependence on God for everything, including becoming more humble. Pray that the Holy Spirit would reveal where pride still lurks in your heart and would give you the desire to experience the freedom that humility brings.

UP AHEAD *(5 minutes)*

This is what is ahead in the coming week:

1. Complete the "Put It Together" section below as soon as you can, while your memory of this time is fresh.
2. Between now and the next meeting, read Day 8 through Day 14 of *The Humility Project for Men* devotional. It is all the better if you can read the devotions aloud with one other person. Speaking is good. Each reading is followed by a response. Please don't skip that part.
3. If you haven't asked a person outside the group to pray for you, now is the time.
4. If you already have someone who prays for you, text them after this meeting with what you are learning and how they can pray for you.
5. Talk to *someone* about your humility project—a roommate, friend, spouse, child.
6. Be prepared to mention at the next meeting one thing from the devotions that has been important to you.

PUT IT TOGETHER

How would you summarize your experience during this time? What can you tell others about your humility project this week?

MEETING 3

KNOWING GOD IN JESUS CHRIST—AND RESPONDING

OPENERS *(10 minutes)*

- What one thing from this week's devotionals has been important to you?
- Is someone praying for you? Have you talked with others about what you've been learning? How has that asking and talking been good for your soul?

KEY IDEA

Review: *Humility means that you live before God, dependent on him, with a listening, teachable heart.*

Simply put, humility is submission to your God. Submitting in humility is a result of knowing God well—knowing Jesus well—in his greatness and goodness.

ARTICLE *(5 minutes)*

Knowing the Holy God

Instructions:

- *Read the article aloud, taking turns at the paragraph breaks. If you prefer not to read, say "Pass," and the next person will begin reading.*
- *Sentences in* ***boldface*** *are for the whole group to read aloud together.*

- *If anything from the reading stands out to you, circle, underline, or highlight it. If a question occurs to you, jot it down in the margins. After the reading, you will have an opportunity to share your observations and questions.*

Today you are going into familiar and critical territory. You will consider the greatness and goodness of God, and you will refresh your practice of confession and forgiveness.

The questions are, Who will be bigger? Who will be *magnified*—you or the Lord?

One time you will notice that you need to know the great and good God is when you complain. This week you read about complaining. Good complaining is when you complain *to* God about anything. A good complaint says, "Lord, what you are doing doesn't make any sense and I don't like it." Then, you listen to him, and his words usually remind you about what Jesus has done. For example, he might say, "Do you believe that I care for you? Do you trust me?"

Bad complaining is when you just complain to no one in particular. Pride doesn't always shake its fist at God; it often just grumbles.

So let's start by telling the great and good Lord that we want him to be bigger in our hearts and in what we say.

Oh, magnify the LORD with me,
and let us exalt his name together! (Psalm 34:3)

Knowing God

When comparing notes with a friend about family devotions, I mentioned that our family might pray, read Scripture, and talk about peer pressure or manners. After thinking for a moment about his family's traditions, he said, "We talk about God." I have reflected on his words from then on.

To be a Christian is to know the true God who has revealed himself most fully in Jesus Christ, who entered our world, gathered all kinds of strays to himself, was put to death in his early thirties, rose from the dead in his physical body, now reigns in heaven, and will soon reign on earth. And for a reason we will never fully understand during our time on this earth, God knows you and wants to be known by you. Humility begins by knowing that we live in a Christ-centered world.

Not only is the universe Christ-centered, you are too. At the very depth of the human heart is our need to know the true God (Romans 1:21). Augustine wrote in *Confessions*, "You have made us for yourself, and our hearts are restless until they rest in you."[4] To know God is truly your deepest need.

Jesus Is the Holy God

A central quality of God is holiness. *Holiness* is hard to wrap our minds around, but you might remember the illustrations you read earlier of the cascading avalanche, the crashing wave, the expansive field in a baseball stadium, and the tiny newborn baby. Such things make us stop. God's holiness means that nothing about him is ordinary. He is not only great; he is holy in his greatness.

His love is not like that of a human being; it is holy love. You never quite get fully accustomed to his holiness. It always causes your heart to skip a beat. You pause, you do a double take. You shake your head in wonder as he leaves an indelible imprint. You might feel unworthy when he comes close to you, but it is more that he simply dominates your attention and you can't help but move toward him.

Consider how his holiness leaves its mark in heaven.

> **"Holy, holy, holy, is the Lord God Almighty,**
> **who was and is and is to come!"** (Revelation 4:8)

Then worship breaks out.

Jesus Is Holy in His Power

Jesus is the great and holy God:

> **By him all things were created,**
> **in heaven and on earth, visible and invisible,**
> **whether thrones or dominions or rulers or authorities—**
> **all things were created through him and for him.**
> **And he is before all things, and in him all things hold together.** (Colossians 1:16–17)

In his holy power to create and hold together the universe, Christ is magnified.

But our bad complaining so quickly forgets. Though we seem to complain to no one in particular, our daily grumbling is like a clay pot telling the potter how to run the world.

The Lord once spoke to his people:

> "Woe to him who strives with him who formed him,
> a pot among earthen pots!
> Does the clay say to him who forms it, 'What are you making?'
> or 'Your work has no handles'?" (Isaiah 45:9)

God's people had been grumbling and complaining. And we do the same thing. What we need is the very big and magnified God. Only then does humility grow.

Jesus Is Holy in His Love

God is great in holy power, and he is good in holy love.

> **Power belongs to God,**
> **and . . . to you, O Lord, belongs steadfast love.**
> (Psalm 62:11–12)

The evidence of this steadfast love is that he is pleased to forgive your sins. He desires to keep you close, and forgiveness of sins is essential if you are to be close to the holy God. When you come to him, confessing sin, he never turns you away (John 6:37). Every made-up god requires you to make things right to get into their good graces. Not our Lord: "While we were enemies we were reconciled to God by the death of his Son" (Romans 5:10). All it takes to enter into this love is to know that you are poor and needy. Your life depends on it.

> **If you, LORD, kept a record of sins,**
> **Lord, who could stand?**
> **But with you there is forgiveness,**
> **so that we can, with reverence, serve you.**
> (Psalm 130:3–4 NIV)

Remember: The forgiveness of sins is not first bad news (you're a sinner), then good news (Jesus forgives you). The truth is that the Spirit of God opens your eyes to your sin and need for God's rescue. Only the Spirit can do this, and he does it out of sheer love for you. This is the only way to be rescued. So it is exceptionally good news when you see your own sin. If you don't see that you are a sinner, you don't care that God forgives and rescues because you don't think you need forgiveness or rescue. In that condition, pride is thriving, and it is deadly. *The truly bad news is when you cannot identify any sin in your own life.*

Seeing and confessing your sin is *good.* One result of confessing your sins before the Lord is being less reactive, less sensitive, and less angry when someone criticizes you. Confessing your sins to the Lord robs those criticisms of their power. You have confessed matters that are much more serious than another person's critique, so you are free to listen to what they have to say and discern whether you also need to confess to other people.

It is also good because you no longer have to find your rest in good works or impressing others. You don't have to be somebody, because you have put your trust in Jesus and his reputation, which he shares with you. When you forget, his Spirit shows you the way back.

> **Return, O my soul, to your rest;**
> **for the LORD has dealt bountifully with you.**
> (Psalm 116:7)

A life of humility is about Jesus Christ revealing the Father and sending the Spirit. It's about being amazed that God knows you, and proud that you actually know him and have the privilege of loving him back.

DISCUSSION *(15 minutes)*

How would you describe *holy* to a teen or a child? What passage of Scripture helps you know that Jesus is holy? Does anything else help you know, see, and respond to God's holiness?

To see sin is a gift; to confess is holy. What makes confession of sin hard for you? Is it bad memories, an inaccurate view of God, or examining only outward behavior, rather than inner motives and attitudes? Why is it so hard to acknowledge the obvious to God?

What else stood out to you as we read the article? What questions did you have?

EXERCISE *(20 minutes)*

Instructions:

Read the introductory paragraph together. Then individually answer the questions and pray. Finally, discuss together what you found.

Scripture gives us a specific way to respond in humility to the Lord's greatness. We need to say, "*If the Lord wills,* we will live and do this or that" (James 4:15, emphasis added). Or, "Your will be done." This attitude will prepare you for the inevitable frustrations in the next twenty-four hours.

- Think back to a time in the last week or so when you were full of complaints and frustration because something didn't go your way. Describe briefly what happened.

- How would your response to that situation have been different if you had said in your heart, "If the Lord wills," or, "Your will be done"?

- How do you think remembering to do this will affect your day-to-day life?

- Take time to confess that you don't have a habit of praying, "Lord, if it is your will." Now take time to pray, "*Lord, if it is your will*, this is what I hope to do today and tomorrow. But I submit to your will."

Now take a few minutes to discuss together what you learned.

RESPONSIVE READING AND QUESTIONS *(15 minutes)*

Instructions:

- *React to what you have been learning by reading the following corporate confession responsively. A leader (a volunteer or the group's facilitator) will read the regular text, and the entire group will follow by reading the* **boldface text** *together. You do not need to read the Bible references in parentheses.*
- *As you read, circle, underline, or highlight things that are important to you.*

☙ ☙ ☙

The Lord has promised mercy through Jesus Christ to all who repent and believe in him. Therefore, we confess that we, indeed, have sinned in thought, word, and deed.

Lord, you test our hearts so that we can see our hearts and turn to you.

I have grumbled and complained about people and circumstances, and my grumbling was against you. Lord, forgive me.

In Christ, we have the secret to contentment because you, Lord, have given us all good things.

But my soul can desire more—more things, more love from others, more respect, more money. And I can love all these more than I love you. Lord, forgive me.

You are the God of steadfast love.

But I do not love when other people do not love me well. Lord, forgive me.

The LORD is gracious and merciful, slow to anger and abounding in steadfast love. (Psalm 145:8)

As far as the east is from the west,
so far has he removed our transgressions from us.
As a father has compassion on his children,
so the LORD has compassion on those who fear him.
(Psalm 103:12–13 NIV)

May all who seek you
rejoice and be glad in you;
may those who love your salvation
say continually, **"Great is the LORD!"** (Psalm 40:16)

QUESTIONS

You were asked to circle, underline, or highlight what was important to you. What did you mark and why? What are your initial reactions to this reading?

The reading on secret sins (Day 9) encouraged you to bring any secret sin to the Lord and to speak to a trustworthy Christian about it. There are many stories of people who chose to be transparent and are now living openly before God and others. What ideas do you have on how your community can welcome the confession of hidden sins so that believers can walk in the light?

PRAY *(5 minutes)*

Pray together, praising God for how great and good he is in his holiness. Thank him that both his power and love were on display in Jesus, and express your gratitude for the forgiveness we receive again and again in Christ.

UP AHEAD *(5 minutes)*

This is what is ahead in the coming week:

1. Complete the "Put It Together" section below as soon as you can, while your memory of this time is fresh.
2. Between now and the next meeting, read Day 15 through Day 21 of *The Humility Project for Men* devotional. It is all the better if you can read the devotions aloud with one other person. Speaking is good. Each reading is followed by a response. Please don't skip that portion.
3. After this meeting, text the person who is praying for you to let them know what you are learning and how they can pray for you specifically.
4. Talk to *someone* about your humility project—a roommate, friend, spouse, child.
5. Be prepared to mention at the next meeting one thing from the devotions that has been important to you.

PUT IT TOGETHER

How would you summarize your experience during this time? What one discovery will stick with you? What can you tell others about your humility project this week?

MEETING 4
LIVING HUMBLY BEFORE GOD

OPENERS *(10 minutes)*

- What has been helpful for your soul from this week's readings in the devotional?
- On Day 16, you created two lists of thanks: one of three physical blessings you can see and the other of three spiritual blessings you can't see. Talk about your lists and be inspired by them.

KEY IDEA

Humility means that you live before God, dependent on him, with a listening, teachable heart. As you grow in humility, you will be more aware of and thankful for spiritual blessings. You will be less wrapped up in your abilities, successes, or stuff. And you will have more and more in common with a humble child, tax collector, and servant.

So far in our journey we have done the following:

- You have asked for prayer.
- You are talking.
- You can define *humility* and *pride*, with personal illustrations of both.
- You know why we have worked to know Jesus as holy in both his greatness and his love.
- You have spoken with somebody about what you are learning.
- You are getting the knack of "I am poor and needy."

ARTICLE *(5 minutes)*

Facets of Humility

Instructions:

- *Read the article aloud, taking turns at the paragraph breaks. If you prefer not to read, say "Pass," and the next person will begin reading.*
- *Sentences in* **boldface** *are for the whole group to read aloud together.*
- *If anything from the reading stands out to you, circle, underline, or highlight it. If a question occurs to you, jot it down in the margins. After the reading, you will have an opportunity to share your observations and questions.*

We've talked about how in its essence being humble is living before God, dependent on him, with a listening, teachable heart. Humility leads us to new ways of acting and speaking, and even new ways of being. Consider some of its fruits.

Giving Thanks for Spiritual Blessings

Let's start with thanksgiving. "What do you have that you did not receive?" (1 Corinthians 4:7). Pride thinks we deserve good things; humility knows they are gifts. These gifts are *spiritual* because they come from the Spirit, and we see them because the Spirit gives us eyes to see what is most important and eternal. "For the things that are seen are transient, but the things that are unseen are eternal" (2 Corinthians 4:18).

This week you created two different lists of thanks: three things that you see physically and three things you don't. For things that you *see*, you may have noted ways God has provided for your needs. However, these things can fade, depending on the day. The things you see by faith—no more sin barrier separating you from God, and the light of his presence now—are always there, and thanksgiving is always an appropriate response.

As we give thanks, new identities begin to take shape. We see pride more clearly, in our grumbling and judgments on others, and we are willing to cast it aside. We also take to heart some identities we never would have imagined, such as a child, tax collector, or servant.

Knowing Who You Are

Here are two identities that are on their way out:

Grumbler. While good complaining speaks what is on your heart to the Lord, bad complaining is grumbling about whatever you don't like to yourself or anyone other than the Lord. Scripture makes a big deal out of bad complaining, partly because it feels so normal to us.

Achiever. Pride can hide in resumes and reputation. *Your perceived successes pose great danger.* They can deceive you into thinking there are areas of your life where you can say, "I've got this—I don't need God's help." You can go for days without seeming to need Jesus, and prideful judgment of others is sure to follow.

Just as with the burdens of sin, regrets, and shame, we also need to be freed from our accomplishments—freed from the burden of building and maintaining our identities around them or using them to measure ourselves and others. Cling instead to spiritual things, "the good portion, which will not be taken away from [you]" (Luke 10:42).

The apostle Paul took a radical approach to anything that left room for self-trust: It is highly toxic. Discard it. Quickly. Run from it. He understood from his own experience how we quickly rely on our personal abilities, accomplishments, or reputation. He does not demean gifts and good works. Paul is instead concerned about our tendency to *trust* in those accomplishments.

In his letter to the Philippians, Paul first reviews his achievements, lineage, and education—all the things he once rested in.

> If anyone else thinks he has reason for confidence in the flesh, I have more: circumcised on the eighth day, of the

> people of Israel, of the tribe of Benjamin, a Hebrew of Hebrews; as to the law, a Pharisee; as to zeal, a persecutor of the church; as to righteousness under the law, blameless. (Philippians 3:4–6)

This is what the Philippians were hoping for—an accomplished church planter who could enhance their prestige. Then Paul throws his accomplishments in the trash, "count[ing] them as rubbish" (Philippians 3:8). Without this burden he is free to enter into joy, "because of the surpassing worth of knowing Christ Jesus my Lord" (Philippians 3:8). He has found the greatest of all gifts (Matthew 13:44) and could now live out new identities.

Here are three identities that are on their way in:

Child. The identity of *child* is awkward. But remember that we're focused on life with God. In that relationship, you are most certainly a child. You are God's offspring by creation, a renegade by sin, and an adopted child by grace. You might prefer *son of God*, which at least sounds like you are a maturing teen rather than a child, but the apostle John prefers the words *child* and *children*: "To all who did receive [Christ], who believed in his name, he gave the right to become children of God" (John 1:12).

Your Father cares for you, so you can rest in him. The apostle Peter encourages us in this:

> Humble yourselves, therefore, under the mighty hand of God so that at the proper time he may exalt you, casting all your anxieties on him, because he cares for you. (1 Peter 5:6–7)

In other words, a child talks about his fears to his father. A child knows that he is quite small, the mighty God is his Father, and that cares are best left to him.

Tax collector. This identity is introduced to us by Jesus. Its larger category is people who are scorned by others or perceived as being less than others. With the identity of tax collector, you adopt an identity that's distinctly unimpressive.

> [Jesus] also told this parable to some who trusted in themselves that they were righteous, and treated others with contempt: "Two men went up into the temple to pray, one a Pharisee and the other a tax collector. The Pharisee, standing by himself, prayed thus: 'God, I thank you that I am not like other men, extortioners, unjust, adulterers, or even like this tax collector. I fast twice a week; I give tithes of all that I get.' But the tax collector, standing far off, would not even lift up his eyes to heaven, but beat his breast, saying, 'God, be merciful to me, a sinner!' I tell you, this man went down to his house justified, rather than the other. For everyone who exalts himself will be humbled, but the one who humbles himself will be exalted." (Luke 18:9–14)

Here is the classic distinction between the proud and the humble: The man who is proud rests on his accomplishments and uses them to give himself a boost over others, while the man who is humble knows his neediness before God and doesn't compare himself to other people.

Servant. Wise men throughout history have aspired to this third identity. However, this desire has fallen out of style because we think of being an oppressed servant of other people rather than a servant of God. The reality, of course, is that you either live under the deadly and oppressive masters of sin, Satan, and death, or you live under the humble King. This servant identity is especially important when God calls you to obey and you are not quite persuaded that you want to actually obey (think about lies that don't seem to hurt anyone, or all things sexual). A servant doesn't ignore his master's commands when they are inconvenient or contrary to his desires. A servant says, "Speak, LORD, for your servant hears" (1 Samuel 3:9).

DISCUSSION *(15 minutes)*

Notice any grumbling and bad complaining recently? Any thoughts on how to battle them?

Paul takes an aggressive approach to those items on his resume that give him a little pride in himself and leave him less dependent on God. What items on your resume shape your identity? (Where are you a bit oversensitive to criticism?) What could be your own method to "count them as rubbish" (Philippians 3:8)?

As a way to work your skills, can you add one more item to your list of spiritual blessings?

EXERCISE *(20 minutes)*

Instructions:

In the left-hand column of the table, check the proud thoughts and tendencies that you struggle with the most. In the right-hand column, check the thoughts and qualities that you would most like to be true of you.

Discuss your findings as a group.

THE PROUD

PHARISEE, or
PAUL (SAUL) BEFORE HE MET CHRIST

- ☐ I have categories in my head of "not so bad" sins and "really bad" sins.
- ☐ I tend to compare myself with someone "worse."
- ☐ I grumble when things don't go my way.
- ☐ When I do something good, I hope other people notice.
- ☐ I don't feel a strong need to ask God for forgiveness.
- ☐ I sometimes just go through the religious motions of prayer or worship.
- ☐ As a Christian, I sometimes feel like I'm more sensible or enlightened than people around me who don't have faith in Christ.
- ☐ I use my resume to lift me up when I am down.

THE HUMBLE

CHILD

- ☐ Knows he is weak and limited and merely human—and that's okay
- ☐ Knows he needs to depend on his Father
- ☐ Knows he cannot fix everything himself
- ☐ Does not try to control or manipulate people or events
- ☐ Brings his needs and anxieties to God in prayer
- ☐ Knows how much God cares for him
- ☐ Is able to rest in God despite hard circumstances

SERVANT

- ☐ Is content to live under the humble King, and trusts his character
- ☐ Doesn't try to be impressive
- ☐ Seeks God's will through Scripture and prayer
- ☐ Desires to obey even when it's hard or doesn't seem to make sense

TAX COLLECTOR

- ☐ Doesn't compare himself with others
- ☐ Sees his own sin
- ☐ Knows he needs God's mercy and asks for it

Among the humble identities, which one is especially helpful for you and why?

Given what has been important to you from these lists, what do you want to ask for that only God can give?

Take a few minutes to share your findings.

RESPONSIVE READING AND QUESTIONS *(15 minutes)*

Instructions:

- *Read the following servant songs responsively. The first one, from Isaiah, looks ahead to Jesus, the Messiah and ultimate Servant of God. The second, from Philippians, describes the humility of the eternal Son, who became a lowly servant. A leader (a volunteer or the group's facilitator) will read the regular text, and the entire group with read the* **boldface text** *together. You do not need to read the Bible references in parentheses.*
- *As you read, circle, underline, or highlight things that tell you what Jesus the Servant is like.*

ও ও ও

Isaiah writes of the Suffering Servant:

He had no beauty or majesty to attract us to him,
nothing in his appearance that we should desire him.

He was despised and rejected by mankind,
a man of suffering, and familiar with pain.

Like one from whom people hide their faces
he was despised, and we held him in low esteem.

Surely he took up our pain
and bore our suffering,
yet we considered him punished by God,
stricken by him, and afflicted.

But he was pierced for our transgressions,
he was crushed for our iniquities;
the punishment that brought us peace was on him,
and by his wounds we are healed.

We all, like sheep, have gone astray,
each of us has turned to our own way;
and the Lord has laid on him
the iniquity of us all.

He was oppressed and afflicted,
yet he did not open his mouth;
he was led like a lamb to the slaughter,
and as a sheep before its shearers is silent,
so he did not open his mouth.

By oppression and judgment he was taken away.
Yet who of his generation protested?
For he was cut off from the land of the living;
for the transgression of my people he was punished. . . .

Yet it was the Lord's will to crush him and cause him to suffer,
and though the Lord makes his life an offering for sin,
he will see his offspring and prolong his days,
and the will of the Lord will prosper in his hand.
After he has suffered,
he will see the light of life and be satisfied. . . .

Therefore I will give him a portion among the great,
and he will divide the spoils with the strong,
because he poured out his life unto death,
and was numbered with the transgressors.
For he bore the sin of many,
and made intercession for the transgressors.
(Isaiah 53:2–8, 10–12 NIV)

In Philippians, Paul gives us the big picture of the life of Jesus:

Who, being in very nature God,
did not consider equality with God something to be used to his own advantage;
rather, he made himself nothing
by taking the very nature of a servant,
being made in human likeness.

And being found in appearance as a man,
he humbled himself
by becoming obedient to death—
even death on a cross!

Therefore God exalted him to the highest place
and gave him the name that is above every name,
that at the name of Jesus every knee should bow,
in heaven and on earth and under the earth,
and every tongue acknowledge that Jesus Christ is Lord,
to the glory of God the Father.
(Philippians 2:6–11 NIV)

QUESTIONS

What is Jesus the Servant like, according to these passages?

What *pattern* do you see in the life of the Servant Jesus in both passages?

PRAY *(5 minutes)*

Pray together that the gifts you've been given would fill you with thankfulness rather than pride and that, like the child, the servant, and the tax collector, you would find your identity in dependence on your heavenly Father.

UP AHEAD *(5 minutes)*

This is what is ahead in the coming week:

1. Complete the "Put It Together" section below as soon as you can, while your memory of this time is fresh.
2. Between now and the next meeting, read Day 22 through Day 28 of *The Humility Project for Men* devotional. Don't forget to do the response that follows each reading.
3. After this meeting, talk to or text the person who is praying for you. Tell them about the exercise you did, and ask them to pray about the ways you want to grow in humility.
4. Talk to *someone* about your humility project—a roommate, friend, spouse, child.
5. Be prepared to mention at the next meeting one thing from the devotions that has been important to you.

PUT IT TOGETHER

You have considered some weighty topics: thanks for spiritual gifts, how your successes pose the greatest danger, and new identities. How would you summarize what has been important for you during these times and in the readings?

If you have time, go through this list of what humility looks and feels like. Feel free to add to this list.

- Since humility holds all virtues together, you know that God's call to humility is another way of inviting you to know him and love him.
- You can feel inadequate and be okay with it. Next step? To see inadequacy as an opportunity to know humble strength and trust.
- You think about God more often.
- You talk with him more often. Prayer is an accurate gauge for humility.
- You notice that humility has found a place in your thoughts.
- You have had a few conversations about humility.
- You see the possibilities for being more settled in who you are and who you are not. You are almost okay with the idea of not being somebody special.
- You listen more carefully to sermons.
- You sing a little louder during worship.
- You can identify one area of sin that the Spirit has shown you.
- You can give a few descriptions or definitions of humility.
- You remember at least five of the daily devotions in the book we are studying.
- You have given thanks to the Lord for *spiritual* blessings in the past week.
- You had the courage to talk to the Lord about your troubles and hardships.
- If you are married, your wife is glad that you are reading this.
- ______________________________
- ______________________________
- ______________________________

Do you have any questions?

MEETING 5
LIVING HUMBLY IN RELATIONSHIPS WITH OTHERS

OPENERS *(10 minutes)*

- What has been important to you in the readings? What have you been talking about?
- Have you been aware of "in all humility" as you go through your day? What has the Spirit been doing in you?

KEY IDEA

Humility is submission to God. It means that you walk with God, always needing him, resting in him, and hearing his words. Then you go into the streets with the hope that humility will be on display in your relationships in simple, God-honoring ways. Humility is walking with the Servant-King, *like* the Servant-King, for the good of others and the unity of God's people.

In this week's devotions, you considered humility before other people. Humility is now going public. You want it to be noticed by both human beings and heavenly beings (Ephesians 3:10). No light under a basket here. "Let your light shine before others, so that they may see your good works and give glory to your Father who is in heaven" (Matthew 5:16). Pride and its associates (the world, the flesh, and the devil) separate people; humility brings people together. In conflicts and tense relationships humility's power is most on display.

ARTICLE *(5 minutes)*

Being Right, Getting Angry, and Needing Forgiveness

Instructions:

- *Read the article aloud, taking turns at the paragraph breaks. If you prefer not to read, say "Pass," and the next person will begin reading.*
- *Sentences in* **boldface** *are for the whole group to read aloud together.*
- *If anything from the reading stands out to you, circle, underline, or highlight it. If a question occurs to you, jot it down in the margins. After the reading, you will have an opportunity to share your observations and questions.*

Being Right

I could describe my own pride in any number of ways: Loving myself above all others, turning away from God, holding God in contempt, or wanting to be somebody but without the hassles of actually being *too* important. Most often, my pride wants to be right. It took me far too long to be undone by this. I have been a counselor and teacher whose job was considering how Scripture speaks about God and the details of daily life. I am not argumentative by nature. I have been on the losing end of endless votes, as an elder, instructor, and father (we had cats, usually two at a time, and I always voted against inviting animals in the house). But the occasional conflicts with my wife can always find either their cause or their fuel in me feeling a little righter than she is. Yes, I would ask forgiveness, often after she did. Then it would come out again a month or so later in the same script, as if it were on an infinite loop in my heart.

But did I love? That question can get to our hearts. This verse speaks about it:

> **Do nothing from selfish ambition or conceit, but in humility count others more significant than yourselves.** (Philippians 2:3)

But pride is clever. We can think we are doing what is best for the other person. "But did I love?" When that question falls short, there is another to consider: Did I listen? Did I listen in a way that she knew I listened and understood her? That last question is bound to bring us up short.

Then humility and love can turn its attention from your heart to your relationship. Ask gently:

> "Could we talk? You seem a little edgy. What's happening?"
>
> "Something bothered me about what you said. Could we talk about it?"

Humility is not silence. It is wisdom that is careful with words and timing. Yes, there are times to overlook slights, but if a matter arises that could in any way linger and separate people, we know that the culture of God's house is to talk. In the worst-case scenario, we can't get through it. Then we pray together and try it again. If we are still stuck, we ask someone else for prayer and help.

Getting Angry

Anger shows us pride's go-to style.

> **What causes quarrels and what causes fights among you? Is it not this, that your passions are at war within you? You desire and do not have, so you murder.** (James 4:1–2)

We are all familiar with anger. Sometimes anger is obvious, and sometimes it's subtle: murder, violence, hatred, yelling, arguing, cursing, conflict, blame, revenge, irritability, jealousy, slander, gossip, schadenfreude, sarcasm, grumbling and bad complaining, and withdrawal and silence.

It points and blames: "You *made* me angry." Apologies are littered with the word *but.*

This kind of anger is the mark of pride. As James tells us, it boils down to me *wanting* something—even *deserving* something—and not getting it. This is completely different from the holy anger we see from Jesus. Jesus's anger is not rooted in *I want*; Jesus is firmly committed to *Thy will be done*. He does not get angry when he is the one sinned against; he gets angry when the weak are oppressed or denied access to God.

Our prideful, self-focused anger is a sign that we have turned from God to our own idols. We love something more than we love Jesus. It is the devil's murderous language. And since the devil is a *lying* murderer (John 8:44), our anger is usually accompanied by deceit. We think: I have a right to judge; I am better than the other person; their sins are worse; they "made" me angry. Or, "I am right."

God gives us a way back. He earnestly *wants* us back.

> **Return to the LORD your God,**
> **for he is gracious and merciful,**
> **slow to anger, and abounding in steadfast love.** (Joel 2:13)

Humility and freedom begin here.

Asking Forgiveness of Others

Humility is happy to confess sin to the Lord. That's what poor and needy people do. Confession is a kind of offering to Jesus. "The sacrifices of God are a broken spirit; a broken and contrite heart, O God, you will not despise" (Psalm 51:17).

When you make that offering of confession, your mind considers the state of your relationships.

> **If you are offering your gift at the altar and there remember that your brother has something against you, leave your gift there before the altar and go. First be reconciled to your brother, and then come and offer your gift.** (Matthew 5:23–24)

After confessing to God and seeking his forgiveness, the next step is to confess to the person you sinned against and seek their forgiveness. After confessing your sin to the Lord, you would think that confessing to a mere human would be easy. And, someday, it will be. For now, it might take some work. It will take even more work if the other person responds with less admiration for your confession than you might hope.

Yes, the entire process is beyond your ability to manage on your own. Every step reminds you this is a spiritual battle. You need the Spirit to bring his life into your soul. Ask the Lord to tame your tendency toward being right, being angry, and wanting what you don't have. The Spirit is glad to do it. And be sure to ask others to pray the same for you. Then watch as, over time, God works in you the qualities we read about in Ephesians, the qualities we see in Jesus: "humility and gentleness, with patience, bearing with one another in love" (4:2).

DISCUSSION *(15 minutes)*

Look again at the list of ways that anger manifests itself. In what ways do you tend to express anger?

What is the general state of your confession to other people? For example, *do you* confess your sin to those you have wronged?

How do you ask forgiveness?

How do you *want* to ask forgiveness?

What else stood out to you as we read the article? What questions did you have?

EXERCISE *(20 minutes)*

Instructions:

Do the exercise on your own. Then discuss with the group something that you learned.

"Knowledge puffs up, but love builds up" (1 Corinthians 8:1 CSB). Paul's words to the Corinthians are good for anyone who has ever felt superior because they are "more right" than someone else or has more knowledge or skill than someone else.

Look over the following list. In what area(s) do you tend to see yourself as being "more right" than certain other people? Check any that apply, and feel free to add your own areas.

- ☐ Theology or Bible knowledge
- ☐ Church service (how sermon, music, etc. should be done)

- ☐ Parenting (discipling, discipline, diet, media consumption, sleep or potty training, education, etc.)
- ☐ Politics
- ☐ General knowledge (history, science, grammar, culture, etc.)
- ☐ Practical things (how to drive or find your way around, how to maintain a home/yard/car, how to calculate a tip in your head, etc.)
- ☐ Other: ________________________________
- ☐ Other: ________________________________

Choose an area that you checked above and answer the following questions with that area in mind.

1. Why is this particular need to be right so important to you? Is there anything that has made you more vulnerable? Your response could consider both your own history (the examples of others, or how you have been treated in the past) and your heart.

2. In your own words and God's words, what helps you loosen your desire to be right? Don't settle for saying things that are true. Settle for words that are good and persuasive to your soul.

Imagine how life would be different if you had less concern about being right and having rights. This hope can guide how you pray and ask others to pray.

Take a few minutes to share something you learned.

RESPONSIVE READING AND QUESTIONS *(15 minutes)*

Instructions:

- *Read the Bible verses below from James and 1 Corinthians. A leader (a volunteer or the group's facilitator) will read the regular text, and the entire group will read the* ***boldface text*** *together. You do not need to read the Bible references in parentheses.*
- *As you read, circle, underline, or highlight things that are important to you. You might especially want to pay attention to the language used in this modern paraphrase, which probably sounds a little different from what you're used to.*

ເ ເ ເ

From James:

Where do you think all these appalling wars and quarrels come from? Do you think they just happen? Think again. They come about because you want your own way, and fight for it deep inside yourselves. You lust for what you don't have and are willing to kill to get it. You want what isn't yours and will risk violence to get your hands on it.

You wouldn't think of just asking God for it, would you? And why not? Because you know you'd be asking for what you have no right to. You're spoiled children, each wanting your own way.

You're cheating on God. If all you want is your own way, flirting with the world every chance you get, you end up enemies of God and his way. And do you suppose God doesn't care? The proverb has it that "he's a fiercely jealous lover." And what he gives in love is far better than anything else you'll find. It's common knowledge that "God goes against the willful proud; God gives grace to the willing humble."

So let God work his will in you. Yell a loud *no* to the Devil and watch him make himself scarce. Say a quiet *yes* to God and he'll be there in no time. Quit dabbling in sin. Purify your inner life. Quit playing the field. Hit bottom, and cry your eyes out. The fun and games are over. Get serious, really serious. Get down on your knees before the Master; it's the only way you'll get on your feet. (James 4:1–10 MSG)

From 1 Corinthians:

If I speak in the tongues of men and of angels, but have not love, I am a noisy gong or a clanging cymbal.

And if I have prophetic powers, and understand all mysteries and all knowledge, and if I have all faith, so as to remove mountains, but have not love, I am nothing.

If I give away all I have, and if I deliver up my body to be burned, but have not love, I gain nothing.

Love is patient and kind; love does not envy or boast; it is not arrogant or rude.

It does not insist on its own way; it is not irritable or resentful; it does not rejoice at wrongdoing, but rejoices with the truth.

Love bears all things, believes all things, hopes all things, endures all things. (1 Corinthians 13:1–7)

QUESTIONS

What did you circle/underline/highlight and why? Did reading the modern paraphrase of James give you any new insights into that passage?

Some of what James says here may sound pretty extreme—wars, violence, fighting, lust, spoiled children. How do you react to such things? Why? Do the things he describes seem to apply to you? Why or why not?

How is love the opposite?

PRAY *(5 minutes)*

Ask the Holy Spirit to be at work in you to make you less angry, less eager to puff yourself up, and more ready to build others up in love. Pray for the humility to ask others for forgiveness when you fail to love them.

UP AHEAD *(5 minutes)*

This is what is ahead in the coming week:

1. Complete the "Put It Together" section below as soon as you can, while your memory of this time is fresh.
2. Between now and the next meeting, read Day 29 through Day 35 of *The Humility Project for Men* devotional. It is all the better if you read the devotions aloud with one other person. Speaking is good. Each reading is followed by a response. Please don't skip that part.
3. After this meeting, text the person who is praying for you. Let them know what you are learning and how they can pray for you.

4. Talk to *someone* about your humility project—a roommate, friend, spouse, child.
5. Be prepared to mention at the next meeting one thing from the devotions that has been important to you.

PUT IT TOGETHER

How would you summarize your experience during this time? What is one thing that will stick with you? What can you tell others about your humility project this week?

MEETING 6
AVOIDING SHAME

OPENERS *(10 minutes)*

- What has been sticking with you over the last few weeks?
- How has humility broken into new areas of your life?

KEY IDEA

We have settled into two definitions of humility. The first identified humility before the Lord.

> *Humility is submission to God that listens to him.*

The second definition extended this idea into daily life.

> *Humility means that you walk with God, needing him, resting in him, always eager to hear his words. Then your humility goes out into the street in hopes that it will be on display in your relationships, in ways that are simple and honoring to the God who serves us. Humility is to walk with the Servant-King, like the Servant-King, for the good of others and the unity of God's people.*

Today, we will further our discussion of humility by looking at shame, a killer of relationships.

ARTICLE *(5 minutes)*

Shame

Instructions:

- *Read the article aloud, taking turns at the paragraph breaks. If you prefer not to read, say "Pass," and the next person will begin reading.*
- *Sentences in* ***boldface*** *are for the group to read aloud together.*
- *If anything from the reading stands out to you, circle, underline, or highlight it. If a question occurs to you, jot it down in the margins. After the reading, you will have an opportunity to share your observations and questions.*

Among men, the topic of shame can take the life out of any conversation. Sometimes we know it's there, but we don't have words for it. Other times we simply want to avoid it. Yet, ignore it or deny it, shame will have its day. "Unacceptable" will pursue you at work and in relationships. It pursues you because you live with something you have done that you believe is unacceptable. The worst of shame, however, comes when other people have humiliated you—treated you like you are nothing—through their words and actions. The resulting shame can be the most life dominating.

Okay so far? Choose one:

"Yes" or **"No"** (If "no," be sure to talk about it.)

Why include shame in a discussion about humility? Because shame can keep you from enjoying the blessings of a safe, humble relationship with God.

- Shame avoids humility because shame makes you feel low, and humility sounds like you have to go lower still.
- Shame makes you deaf to most anything good, such as God's good words to you. It inevitably lies about who you are and who God is. After all, you could not *really* belong to God, it says. You are unlovable.

Let's address these tendencies.

Humility and humiliation. We know that humility is good and necessary if we want a full life. Remember, it is about being under the only good King. Humility should sound very good. We also know that when one person disgraces or harms another, this is loathsome to God, and he will speak compelling and holy words to you that lift you up.

Shame and lies. Shame says that you are eternally unacceptable, unlovable, and unworthy. Other people belong, you do not. As a result, you may see that God's promises and good words are true, but you don't believe they are directed to you. There is no one who cares; there is no one who will help. All these feelings can arise from events that happened years earlier. Shame has no expiration date. Left unattended, it only seems to get bigger and darker with time. Meanwhile, you keep people at a distance and try to present a good front. Even worse, since you have been treated like you are unacceptable, you try to live up to live up to your reputation and *be* unacceptable.

The truth, of course, is that the perpetrator stands under God's judgment (Psalm 35:26), and God's unique interest and care for the rejected and discarded is his standard practice. Think of Joseph's mistreatment by his brothers that was followed by Joseph's line receiving *two* allotments of land. Remember the mistreated women Tamar and Bathsheba being brought into the line of the Messiah, or tax collectors and others who were rejected by society becoming the heroes of God's kingdom. Yet recounting these events is rarely enough to break through the grip of shame.

Open your eyes just a little more. The sins of others are from the anti-kingdom: the world, the flesh, death, and the devil. Don't think that this confederation of darkness is going to let go of a possible victim without a fight, and remember lies are their prominent tactic. Lies are best exposed, mocked, renounced, discarded, and even brought to shame. Your strategy for fighting these lies will sound familiar:

- Talk to the Lord about the war in your soul. If you struggle to find words, try speaking some that you find in Psalms.

- Identify the lies that keep you from coming to the Lord and trusting him.
- Counter falsehood with the cleansing work of Jesus, who himself knew the farthest limits of shame, even becoming cursed for us (Galatians 3:13).
- Find one Scripture that becomes a trusted companion to rescue you when the lies are loud.
- Talk to a wise friend. Shame becomes more vulnerable and less powerful when you bring it out into the open.
- Tell a new story, shaped by the psalms, with God's good words having the final word.

Know this about shame: It loves to be pushed into dark recesses and avoided. You will notice it in how you feel isolated and never quite known by the people who are close to you. This is why God has determined to speak to you over and over about how Jesus entered into shame to take your shame on himself. In this, he separates you from the wretched acts of other people and joins you to himself. Shame is a result of our associations. Your association with Jesus, your new life in him by faith, shatters those old links of shame.

Make Psalm 22 a trusted companion. It begins with Jesus speaking about his shame, and he invites you to join him.

> **My God, my God, why have you forsaken me? Why are you so far from saving me, so far from my cries of anguish? My God, I cry out by day, but you do not answer, by night, but I find no rest.** (Psalm 22:1–2 NIV)

Then, after a struggle, it ends with you as Christ's ambassador to the world.

> **The poor will eat and be satisfied; those who seek the Lord will praise him—may your hearts live forever! All the ends of the earth will remember and turn to the Lord, and all the families of the nations will bow down before him, for dominion belongs to the Lord and he rules over the nations. . . . Posterity will serve him; future**

> **generations will be told about the Lord. They will proclaim his righteousness, declaring to a people yet unborn: He has done it!** (Psalm 22:26–28, 30–31 NIV)

Women have been permitted by the world around them to talk about shame. Men have not. We have heard a few stories of men who acknowledge being sexually abused by priests, but shame usually feels like a weakness too severe to reveal—although men experience it as much as women do. If you have experiences from your past that you want to push away and keep from other people, these are the very things you must speak to Jesus about. Tell him, and then be willing to hear his compassion for you.

DISCUSSION *(15 minutes)*

What do you think of the idea that, in general, society more readily permits women to talk about shame but frowns on men for doing so?

What could you do that would help your community talk about shame?

Why bother speaking openly about shame?

EXERCISE *(20 minutes)*

Instructions:

Answer the questions below on your own. Then take a few minutes to give anyone who would like to share the opportunity to do so.

1. What kinds of situations make you feel shame? (You don't need to delve into deeply painful events right now; we all experience shame in smaller ways, like getting called out for forgetting to do something at work, feeling judged because of something your kid did, or realizing someone heard you say something you didn't want them to hear.)

2. When you feel a wave of shame, what is your instinct? Check as many as apply.
   - ☐ Ignore it. Hide it. Outwardly pretend that whatever it was didn't happen.
   - ☐ Torture yourself by replaying the events in your head.
   - ☐ Berate yourself. Tear yourself down for messing up. Maybe even call yourself names.
   - ☐ Get angry. Escape. Leave as fast as possible.
   - ☐ Make a joke out of the situation.
   - ☐ Blame someone else (either out loud or to yourself).
   - ☐ Try to distract others' attention from it.
   - ☐ Exert yourself to try to prove that you really are good or competent or enough.
   - ☐ Try to avoid the person(s) who witnessed the shameful event(s).
   - ☐ Other: ______________________________

3. Let's dig a little deeper. As we've learned, shame can creep in when we feel we haven't measured up to some standard or to some other person. Sometimes this kind of shame can be a symptom of pride and idolatry. We *want* something—to look smart, competent, athletic, knowledgeable, cool, practical, strong, good at [fill in the blank], laid back, sensitive, etc.—and we failed somehow.

   Do specific *kinds* of failures or mistakes make you cringe to remember them? If so, what are they?

   Why is this particular type of failure so painful? What do you *want* that feels ruined when you mess up in this area?

4. Scan back over the article. List a few specific truths or practices that can help you when shame rears its head.

Now come back together as a group. Would anyone like to share something they learned?

RESPONSIVE READING AND QUESTIONS *(15 minutes)*

Instructions:

- *Read the verses below that speak of our great need and of the Lord's compassion and help. A leader (a volunteer or the group's facilitator) will read the regular text, and the entire group with read the* **boldface text** *together. You do not need to read the Bible references in parentheses.*
- *As you read, circle, underline, or highlight things that are important to you. You might especially want to pay attention to the language used in this modern paraphrase, which probably sounds a little different from what you're used to.*

ଏ ଏ ଏ

Deliver me
    from sinking in the mire;
let me be delivered from my enemies
    and from the deep waters.
Let not the flood sweep over me,
    or the deep swallow me up,
    or the pit close its mouth over me. . . .
You know my reproach,
    and my shame and my dishonor;
    my foes are all known to you.
Reproaches have broken my heart,
    so that I am in despair. . . .
But I am afflicted and in pain;
    let your salvation, O God, set me on high!
    (Psalm 69:14–15, 19–20, 29)

As a father shows compassion to his children,
    so the LORD shows compassion to those who fear him.
For he knows our frame;
    he remembers that we are dust. (Psalm 103:13–14)

A bruised reed he will not break,
    and a faintly burning wick he will not quench;
    he will faithfully bring forth justice. (Isaiah 42:3)

But Zion said, "The LORD has forsaken me;
my Lord has forgotten me."
"Can a woman forget her nursing child,
that she should have no compassion on the son of her womb?
Even these may forget,
yet I will not forget you.
Behold, I have engraved you on the palms of my hands;
your walls are continually before me.
(Isaiah 49:14–16)

When he saw the crowds, he had compassion for them, because they were harassed and helpless, like sheep without a shepherd. (Matthew 9:36)

When he went ashore he saw a great crowd, and he had compassion on them and healed their sick.
(Matthew 14:14)

And when the Lord saw her, he had compassion on her and said to her, "Do not weep." (Luke 7:13)

In my distress I called to the LORD;
I cried to my God for help.
From his temple he heard my voice;
my cry came before him, into his ears. . . .
He reached down from on high and took hold of me;
he drew me out of deep waters. . . .
You save the humble
but bring low those whose eyes are haughty.
You, LORD, keep my lamp burning;
my God turns my darkness into light.
(Psalm 18:6, 16, 27–28 NIV)

I sought the LORD, and he answered me
and delivered me from all my fears.
Those who look to him are radiant,
and their faces shall never be ashamed.
(Psalm 34:4–5)

> And I heard a loud voice from the throne saying, **"Behold, the dwelling place of God is with man. He will dwell with them, and they will be his people, and God himself will be with them as their God. He will wipe away every tear from their eyes, and death shall be no more, neither shall there be mourning, nor crying, nor pain anymore, for the former things have passed away."** (Revelation 21:3–4)

QUESTIONS

Which of these verses can you see being helpful when you feel shame creeping back into your heart?

What did you circle/underline/highlight, and why?

PRAY *(5 minutes)*

Speak to the compassionate God who took your shame upon himself. Ask for the ability to know that his love and promises are for *you* and to live in the freedom knowing that brings.

UP AHEAD *(5 minutes)*

This is what is ahead in the coming week.

1. Complete the "Put It Together" section below as soon as you can, while your memory of this time is fresh.

2. Between now and the next meeting, read Day 36 through Day 42 of *The Humility Project for Men* devotional. Then take the time to also work through the response portion of each devotion.
3. After this meeting, text the person who is praying for you. Let them know what you are learning and how they can pray for you. Include the specific truths or practices you wrote down in the exercise to help you deal with shame in a healthier, freer way.
4. Talk to *someone* about your humility project—a roommate, friend, spouse, child.
5. Be prepared to mention at the next meeting one thing from the devotions that has been important to you.

PUT IT TOGETHER

How would you summarize your experience during this time? What one thing will stick with you? What can you tell others about your humility project this week?

MEETING 7
SPEAKING WORDS THAT BLESS

OPENERS *(10 minutes)*

- In "You First," the Day 41 devotion, you read about how humility is an activist. It rushes into your relationships, work, and worship. You read, "Simple submission to the Lord and neediness before him leads to a life that is fuller and richer, not just busier." Where have you seen this more active style of humility in your life? What stood out to you?
- What stood out to you from the other readings, or from your life as you read, thought, and prayed about these things?

KEY IDEA

Humility is first before God. We depend on him and listen to him. Then we humbly go out into the world and seek to carry loving humility with us into our relationships. This week we'll be looking at how humility cares for others in our daily conversations.

ARTICLE *(5 minutes)*

Humble, Skillful Conversations

Instructions:

- *Read the article aloud, taking turns at the paragraph breaks. If you prefer not to read, say "Pass," and the next person will begin reading.*
- *Sentences in* ***boldface*** *are for the whole group to read aloud together.*

- *If anything from the reading stands out to you, circle, underline, or highlight it. If a question occurs to you, jot it down in the margins. After the reading, you will have an opportunity to share your observations and questions.*
- *Note: This week's "Put It Together" section includes a few questions to help you evaluate how you are doing in the skills discussed in the article.*

Humility will change the way you talk to people. You'll want to grow in your daily conversations so you can enjoy, love, and pray for those around you.

Each person is complex. We are all a jumble of the people, places, and things that have impacted and shaped our lives, for both good and bad. Any of these can be an important part of our conversations. If they are important to the people we speak with, they are important to us. Then you zoom in on the heart. This is where you interact with people most deeply.

The way into the heart is usually through the emotions. These signal what is important to you—what you love, enjoy, desire, prefer, avoid, fear, and loathe. Many psalms reflect this level of the heart in which God implicitly asks, What has been important to you this week—good things, hard things? What's been on your heart? Let's consider how we can use that knowledge to bless others in conversation.

Ways to Bless Others in Conversation

Be interested. Humility can liberate you from self-concern so that you have room to be interested in others. Otherwise, you usually talk about you, while I talk about me. These are soliloquies, more than conversations that draw people together. Even at our best, we often seek out those who share our interests and are easy to talk with. This is natural, but it lacks insight into how life works in God's house. There, words are what we use to know, love, encourage, help, discover, learn, and come closer.

Listen. Although humility is happy to talk and be known, it prefers that the other person speaks just a little more than you. So you invite others to speak:

> "How are you? I haven't talked with you in a while."
>
> "How has your week been?"

When other people talk, you listen for what excites them (what they love) and what distresses them.

A woman poured her heart out to her husband about his neglect and her aloneness, about ways he had pushed their children away. When she stopped talking, he was silent. Granted, after so many words it's hard to know where to start, but she also made what was important quite clear. He finally responded, "I guess I should fix the toilet." He picked up on something unimportant she had said, and his response left her feeling more alone and hopeless.

We, too, have missed people. The way out of this deafness is to believe that the person talking is actually saying something important, and be eager to hear their message. From there, find out what was most painful. What was best? Then, *listening doesn't count until you have said something that shows you both heard and care.* Perhaps you respond, "That was so hard. I really appreciate you telling me about it." You celebrate what is good and show compassion when life has been painful.

If you don't understand why something is important, you ask:

> "It sounds like your interest in sports is the way you connect with your father. No wonder sports are important to you."
>
> "What is really on your heart in all this? What weighs on you the most?"

I have a friend who is strangely dogmatic about Pepsi. After a few years, I finally asked, "What about Pepsi is so important to you?" He said that his brother, older by ten years, drank Pepsi. He had admired his brother more than anyone, and his brother died when my friend was nine. It only took me two decades to learn this.

Your goal is to be a learner. Keep thinking about how your words and conversations can draw out, build up, and bring others together. Pay attention to who has blessed you with their words. Ask those close to you how you can listen more carefully. Learn from others.

See the good and praiseworthy qualities in people. No doubt many people know you like them, but have you expressed the good you have seen in them? Do they know how they have blessed you? With men, this is rarely the case. Such words seem too personal, if not intimate. But the good needs to be spoken. *If you see the good and don't speak about it, it doesn't count.* Remember that the kingdom of God is filled with endless conversations.

> "I really appreciate how you care for people so well, how your words in a group invite people to be open . . ."
>
> "Thanks so much for . . ."
>
> "Your teaching was so helpful; this is what I did with it . . ."

Like everything else that expresses humility, this work is spiritual. Ask the Spirit to lead you further into these skills.

Pray for others. Remember that you are moving toward something deeper in people. Conversations that are linked to Christ are the best and deepest. And the most natural way to have these conversations is to listen for one thing you can pray about or give thanks for. If the person is clearly burdened and you have no idea how to pray, ask. Nothing is more important than speaking to the God who always hears you.

Then everything changes. You are getting to know the person in their depths. If the setting allows, pray for the person right there. Though initially awkward, once you try it, you will love it. Until then, pray for the person on your own time. Follow up because you want to see what the Spirit is doing.

> "Hey, good to see you. I have been praying for you. Tell me, what's been happening?"

It doesn't count unless *you listen and respond.* After this, conversations are easier and deeper. Everything has changed.

Ask for prayer. Since you are learning about being poor and needy, you also contribute to relationships by asking for prayer. This is harder than praying for someone, so get prepared.

Refrain from giving advice. Your tendency to give advice is the most common conversation killer (see Day 34 on compassion). The ability *not* to speak the advice that pops into your head while someone is talking will help you bless others.

DISCUSSION *(15 minutes)*

Without a compelling reason to change, we all stick with what we do naturally. Why bother being interested in others? How can we cultivate that genuine interest?

What do you want to confess to the Lord about how you listen and care for others? What one small step can you plan to take as you listen and care?

To be able to listen well, you learn skills that invite a person to speak and help draw out the reluctant. Have you met anyone who does that well? What does that person do specifically?

EXERCISE *(20 minutes)*

Instructions:

Do the exercise on your own. Then discuss it as a group.

As a way of remembering and applying what you read this week about conversations, review the article and answer the questions below:

1. On a scale of 1–100, how would you grade yourself as a listener? ______

   What one thing would improve your score?

2. On a scale of 1–100, how would you grade yourself as one who sees and speaks about the good in others? ______

   What one thing would improve your score?

3. On a scale of 1–100, how would you grade yourself on praying for others? ______

   What one thing would improve your score?

4. On a scale of 1–100, how would you grade yourself on asking for prayer? ______

   What one thing would improve your score?

5. On a scale of 1–100, how would you grade yourself on giving advice? (You get a high score when you bite your tongue before you give unsolicited advice.) ______

   What one thing would improve your score?

6. In this meeting we touched on being interested, listening, seeing what is good, and praying, with a brief stop to yell about giving advice. How can you grow in your words and conversations?

Rejoin the group. Share something you learned, and maybe share your plan to grow in your words and conversations.

RESPONSIVE READING AND QUESTIONS *(15 minutes)*

Instructions:

- *This week's responsive reading is a prayer. A leader (a volunteer or the group's facilitator) will read the verses in regular text, and the entire group will respond by reading the* ***boldface*** *prayer together. You do not need to read the Bible references in parentheses.*
- *As you read, circle, underline, or highlight things that are important to you. You might want to pay special attention to the language used in this modern paraphrase, which probably sounds a little different from what you're used to.*

ଓଃ ଓଃ ଓଃ

[Speak] the truth in love. . . . Let no corrupting talk come out of your mouths, but only such as is good for building up, as fits the occasion, that it may give grace to those who hear. (Ephesians 4:15, 29)

If I speak in the tongues of men and of angels, but have not love, I am a noisy gong or a clanging cymbal. (1 Corinthians 13:1)

Lord, fill me with love for others, and give me words to build them up.

Gracious words are like a honeycomb,
sweetness to the soul and health to the body.
(Proverbs 16:24)

Lord, let my words be filled with grace to bless others.

Speak evil of no one, . . . avoid quarreling, . . . be gentle, and . . . show perfect courtesy toward all people. (Titus 3:2)

Lord, help me to be gentle and kind in my interactions with others.

When words are many, transgression is not lacking,
    but whoever restrains his lips is prudent.
The tongue of the righteous is choice silver.
(Proverbs 10:19–20)

Lord, give me the wisdom to know when to speak and when to be quiet.

Let every person be quick to hear, slow to speak. (James 1:19)

Lord, give me the desire and patience to hear what others are saying to me.

If one gives an answer before he hears,
    it is his folly and shame.
A man's spirit will endure sickness,
    but a crushed spirit who can bear?
An intelligent heart acquires knowledge,
    and the ear of the wise seeks knowledge.
        (Proverbs 18:13–15)

Lord, give me the humility to listen and understand.

Bear one another's burdens, and so fulfill the law of Christ. (Galatians 6:2)

Whoever sings songs to a heavy heart is like one who takes off a garment on a cold day, and like vinegar on soda. (Proverbs 25:20)

Rejoice with those who rejoice, weep with those who weep. (Romans 12:15)

Lord, give me grace to know how to respond to people who are burdened, and the generosity of spirit to rejoice with those who rejoice.

Our heart is wide open. (2 Corinthians 6:11)

Lord, enable me to be like Paul, with my heart open to those you have put in my life.

QUESTIONS

What did you circle/underline/highlight, and why?

Which of these verse(s) would you like to hang on to—read again and again, pray over, perhaps memorize?

PRAY *(5 minutes)*

Pray for your conversations. You might confess how you've fallen short in caring for people. Talk to God about your plan to grow in your words and conversations, and ask him to bring about this change in your life.

UP AHEAD *(5 minutes)*

This is what is ahead in the coming week (note that parts of it look different from what you've been asked to do in previous weeks):

1. Complete the "Put It Together" section below as soon as you can, while your memory of this time is fresh.
2. Between now and the next meeting, read "True Manhood," the conclusion of *The Humility Project for Men* devotional.
3. Read back through the story of pride and humility that you wrote at the end of Day 42. Have any new ideas or different perspectives occurred to you since you last looked at it? Be prepared to take about five minutes at the next meeting to

share your story with the men in your group. Again, you can loosely structure your story with these questions:
   - What title fits your story?
   - Who shaped your story? How have they helped or hurt the way you listen to the Lord?
   - How have your strengths and weaknesses and successes and failures shaped your story?
   - When did you notice Jesus come into your story?
   - What are you learning about pride and humility now?
   - How is Jesus becoming larger in your story?
4. After this meeting, text the person who is praying for you. Let them know what you are learning and how they can pray for you. You might also ask them to pray for you as you share your story with the group.
5. Talk to *someone* about your humility project—a roommate, friend, spouse, child.

PUT IT TOGETHER

How would you summarize your experience during this time? What one thing will stick with you? What can you tell others about your humility project this week?

MEETING 8
SHARING OUR STORIES OF PRIDE AND HUMILITY

The format for today's meeting is a little different. Most of the familiar elements are here, but the time is distributed a little differently and the main feature is the stories that participants will share with one another. If your group is large, you might want to break into smaller groups of four or five participants for the storytelling portion of the meeting.

OPENERS *(5 minutes)*

- What stood out to you from "True Manhood," the conclusion of the devotional?
- What stood out from the words of Jesus that were discussed?

KEY IDEA AND STORIES *(25 minutes)*

Humility means that you deny yourself, put pride to death, and are proud to walk with Jesus. One way to practice this and remember that humility is first before God is to say these sentences:

Jesus, I belong to you.
You belong to me.

We've looked at humility from various angles over the last several weeks. This week you finally get to tell others the story you wrote of pride and humility in your own life.

Instructions:

- *Give everyone a chance to tell his story. Aim for five minutes each.*
- *Have at least one person respond to each story, answering questions such as, What do I appreciate from that story? What did I learn?*

ARTICLE *(5 minutes)*

Signposts

Instructions:

- *Read the article aloud, taking turns at the paragraph breaks and bullet points. If you prefer not to read, say "Pass," and the next person will begin reading.*
- *If anything from the reading stands out to you, circle, underline, or highlight it. If a question occurs to you, jot it down in the margins. After the reading, you will have an opportunity to share your observations and questions.*

At some level, of course, this Humility Project has been about change. Yet humility will leave you recognizable to others. If you are outgoing and gregarious, you will still be outgoing and gregarious. But you will be a big personality who cares about the interests of others and is quick to learn from them. If you are an introvert who feels awkward in larger groups and are not prone to small talk, you will listen for what is important for people, talk more, and be less self-conscious because you have a mission. Everyone will laugh more because God is in control and they have freedom to enjoy others.

And there is more. Humility unleashes your natural boldness and openness. Here are a few more signposts as you walk humbly with God:

- Overall, you listen just a little more than you talk.
- You are less cautious about making the first move and taking initiative, while holding your plans loosely and being open to the input of others.
- A daily rhythm emerges. The morning begins, "Let all who take refuge in you rejoice; let them ever sing for joy, and spread your protection over them" (Psalm 5:11). The day ends, "In peace I will both lie down and sleep; for you alone, O LORD,

make me dwell in safety" (Psalm 4:8). Dependence runs through your day.

- You don't give anxiety the last word. Among your last words of the day are, "Everything is as my Father intends."
- You feel secure because of your Father's care, not because of your competencies.
- You are aware of your desire for control, and it is fading.
- You know that humility, boldness, and courage go together. (Can you explain how that works?)
- You know your pride can be very nuanced and parade as goodness. The best way to subdue it is to confess your sins daily.
- You know and work to understand those who are different from you (children, teens, neighbors). You bring interest and curiosity to your relationships.
- You are genuinely appreciative when someone is kind and helpful at a store or restaurant, and you say something to them.
- You receive honor and thanks with grace. You don't say, "It was nothing," but perhaps, "It was my pleasure to do that," or a simple, "Thank you."
- You proceed carefully, even slowly, in more volatile situations.
- You can see good in everyone, and you often point it out. That's what happens when life is no longer about comparing yourself with others.
- When you are criticized, and you either don't see the problem or you disagree, you gently ask the person to help you see the concern.
- You ask forgiveness first, especially when you have been angry. When you do, you also remember that you still want to confess how your sin against another person was against God.
- You know that humility is a deliberate course. Like all growth in Christ, it grows best with consistent focus, prayer, and talking. It is never fully natural.

DISCUSSION *(5 minutes)*

What would you add to this list of signposts?

EXERCISE *(20 minutes)*

Instructions:

In place of the "Put It Together" section you usually find at the end of a session, this will be a kind of overarching "Put It Together" for the entire study. Answer the questions on your own. Then discuss together as a group.

1. Looking back:

   If someone asked you to sum up everything you've studied over the last several weeks in one or two sentences, what would you say?

   What will stick with you?

   What was especially convicting?

2. Looking ahead:

   How do you hope to grow in humility? Be specific.

   What do you expect to find challenging?

Come back together as a group and share some of your thoughts.

RESPONSIVE READING AND QUESTIONS *(10 minutes)*

Instructions:

- *Read the verses below. In general, the regular text exhorts us to become more like Christ, and the* ***boldface text*** *encourages us that God himself works in us to help us change and grow. A leader (a volunteer or the group's facilitator) will read the regular text, and the entire group the* ***boldface text*** *together. No need to read the Bible references in parentheses.*
- *As you read, circle, underline, or highlight things that are important to you.*

ഗ ഗ ഗ

"Come to me, all you who are weary and burdened, and I will give you rest. Take my yoke upon you and learn from me, for I am gentle and humble in heart, and you will find rest for your souls." (Matthew 11:28–29 NIV)

Now the Lord is the Spirit, and where the Spirit of the Lord is, there is freedom. And we all, with unveiled face,

> **beholding the glory of the Lord, are being transformed into the same image from one degree of glory to another. For this comes from the Lord who is the Spirit.**
> (2 Corinthians 3:17–18)

Finally, all of you, have unity of mind, sympathy, brotherly love, a tender heart, and a humble mind. (1 Peter 3:8)

Put on then, as God's chosen ones, holy and beloved, compassionate hearts, kindness, humility, meekness, and patience, bearing with one another and, if one has a complaint against another, forgiving each other; as the Lord has forgiven you, so you also must forgive. And above all these put on love, which binds everything together in perfect harmony. (Colossians 3:12–14)

> **Now may our God and Father himself, and our Lord Jesus, direct our way to you, and may the Lord make you increase and abound in love for one another and for all, as we do for you, so that he may establish your hearts blameless in holiness before our God and Father, at the coming of our Lord Jesus with all his saints.** (1 Thessalonians 3:11–13)

For by the grace given to me I say to everyone among you not to think of himself more highly than he ought to think, but to think with sober judgment, each according to the measure of faith that God has assigned. For as in one body we have many members, and the members do not all have the same function, so we, though many, are one body in Christ, and individually members one of another. (Romans 12:3–5)

> **Let love be genuine. Abhor what is evil; hold fast to what is good. Love one another with brotherly affection. Outdo one another in showing honor. Do not be slothful in zeal, be fervent in spirit, serve the Lord. Rejoice in hope, be patient in tribulation, be constant in prayer. Contribute to the needs of the saints and seek to show hospitality.**
> (Romans 12:9–13)

Rejoice with those who rejoice, weep with those who weep. Live in harmony with one another. Do not be haughty, but associate with the lowly. Never be wise in your own sight. Repay no one evil for evil, but give thought to do what is honorable in the sight of all. If possible, so far as it depends on you, live peaceably with all. (Romans 12:15–18)

Now may the God of peace himself sanctify you completely, and may your whole spirit and soul and body be kept blameless at the coming of our Lord Jesus Christ. He who calls you is faithful; he will surely do it. (1 Thessalonians 5:23–24)

QUESTIONS

What did you circle/underline/highlight, and why?

Exhortation and encouragement go together. How does each affect you?

PRAY *(5 minutes)*

Pray for each member of the group. The stories you heard earlier have probably given you some ideas of things to pray for. You might also use verses from the responsive reading in your prayer.

UP AHEAD

1. After this meeting, text the person who is praying for you. Let them know what you have learned, what you hope to continue to learn, and how they can pray for you.
2. Talk to *someone* about your humility project—a roommate, friend, spouse, child.

ENDNOTES

1. Saint Augustine, "Letter 118," Trans. J. G. Cunningham, in *Nicene and Post-Nicene Fathers*, First Series, Vol. 1. Edited by Philip Schaff (Christian Literature Publishing Co., 1887.) Revised and edited for New Advent website by Kevin Knight, http://www.newadvent.org/fathers/1102118.htm.

2. Eugene Peterson, *Earth and Altar: The Community of Prayer in a Self-Bound Society* (InterVarsity Press, 1985).

3. John Calvin, *The Gospel According to St. John 11–21 & the First Epistle of John*, trans. T. H. L. Parker in *Calvin's New Testament Commentaries*. Edited by David Torrance and Thomas Torrance (Eerdmans, 1959), 254.

4. Augustine, *Confessions*, ed. and trans. Carolyn J.-B. Hammond (Harvard University Press, 2014), 3, https://www.loebclassics.com/view/augustine-confessions_2014/2014/pb_LCL026.3.xml?readMode=recto.

ccef

CCEF is committed to restoring Christ to counseling and counseling to the church. They seek to accomplish this mission through resources, courses, events, and counseling.

To learn more or explore CCEF's resources, visit **ccef.org**.